Easy Learning

JDBC+Oracle

YANG HU

Simple is the beginning of wisdom. From the essence of practice,this book to briefly explain the concept and vividly cultivate programming interest.

http://en.verejava.com

ISBN: 9781095228678

CONTENTS

1. JDBC connect Oracle about CRUD 2

    1.1 Add Data To Table 6

    1.2 Read Data From Table 8

    1.3 Update Data To Table 9

    1.4 Delete Data From Table 11

2. JDBC Precompiled CRUD 13

    2.1 Add Data To Table 14

    2.2 Read Data From Table 16

    2.3 Update Data To Table 17

    2.4 Delete Data From Table 19

3. JDBC Tool DBUtil 21

4. DBUtil User CRUD 25

    4.1 Add Data To Table 26

    4.2 Read Data From Table 27

    4.3 Update Data To Table 28

    4.4 Delete Data From Table 29

5. DBUtil UserDAO CRUD 32

    5.1 Add Data To Table 35

    5.2 Read Data From Table 36

    5.3 Update Data To Table 37

    5.4 Delete Data From Table 38

6. DBUtil UserDAO Paging Query 39

7. JDBC Reflections Any Object 43

8. JDBC Transaction 46

9. JDBC Save and Export Text File 48

10. JDBC Save and Export Picture 53

11. JDBC Call Stored Procedure Add User 57

12. JDBC Call Stored Procedure Update User...59

13. JDBC Call Stored Procedure Delete User..61

14. JDBC Call Stored Procedure Query User 63

15. JDBC Call Stored Procedure Return Parameter 66

JDBC connect Oracle CRUD

If you need to learn Oracle basics, please read my book
<<Easy Learning Oracle SQL>>

https://www.amazon.com/dp/1094789100

1. Download jdbc to connect Oracle driver jar
ojdbc6.jar

 http://en.verejava.com/download.jsp?id=1

2. Open Web isqlplus and login to Oracle with your username/password
http://192.168.1.104:5560/isqlplus

3. create a table: users

```sql
create table users
(
    id numeric,
    username varchar2(100),
    password varchar2(100)
);
```

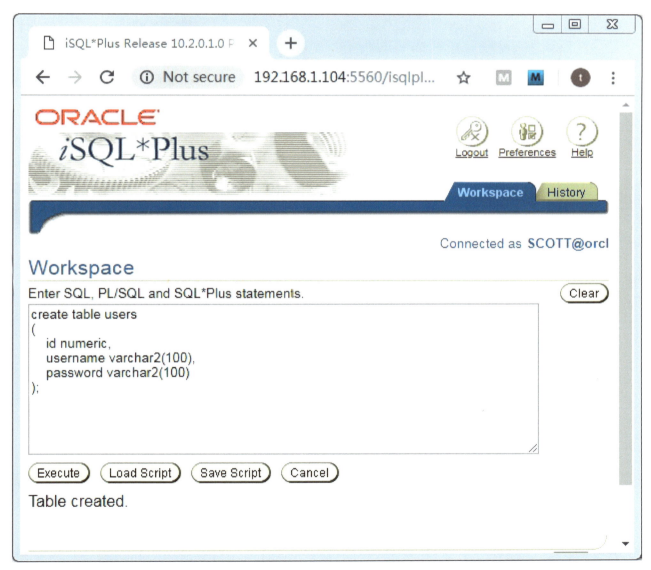

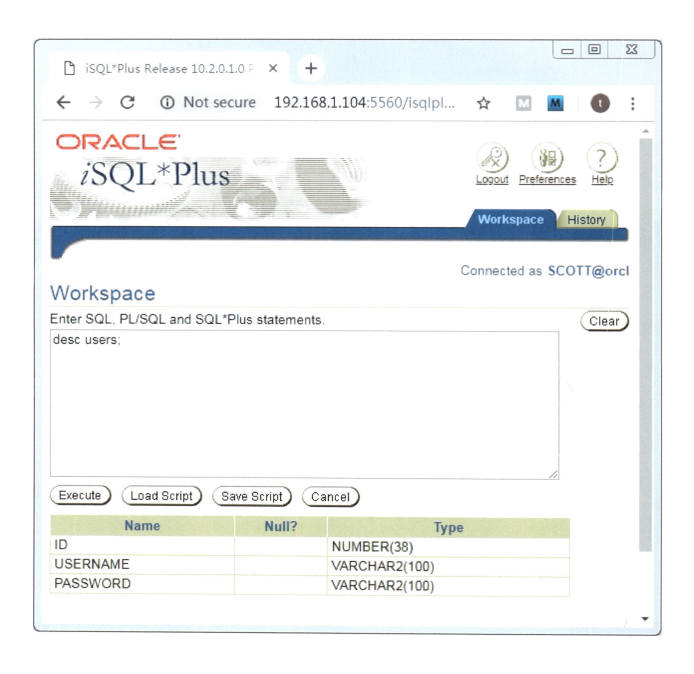

4. Open Eclipse and create a java project jdbc_oracle
Add ojdbc6.jar to **jdbc_oracle** java project

5. Add TestAdd.java to insert data to users table

```java
import java.sql.*;

public class TestAdd {

    public static void main(String[] args) {
        Connection conn = null;
        try {
            // Load jdbc connect Oracle driver by ojdbc6.jar
            Class.forName("oracle.jdbc.driver.OracleDriver");

            //Create connection
            //ip : 192.168.1.104, database name : orcl , username : scott , password : verejava1981
            conn = DriverManager.getConnection("jdbc:oracle:thin:@192.168.1.104:1521:orcl",
"scott", "verejava1981");

            //sql statement insert data to table: users
            String sql = "insert into users(id,username,password)values(1,'David','111111')";

            //Create an Statement that executes the sql
            Statement stmt = conn.createStatement();
            stmt.executeUpdate(sql);

        } catch (Exception e) {
            e.printStackTrace();
        } finally {
            try {
                conn.close();
            } catch (SQLException e) {
                e.printStackTrace();
            }
        }
    }
}
```

Result:

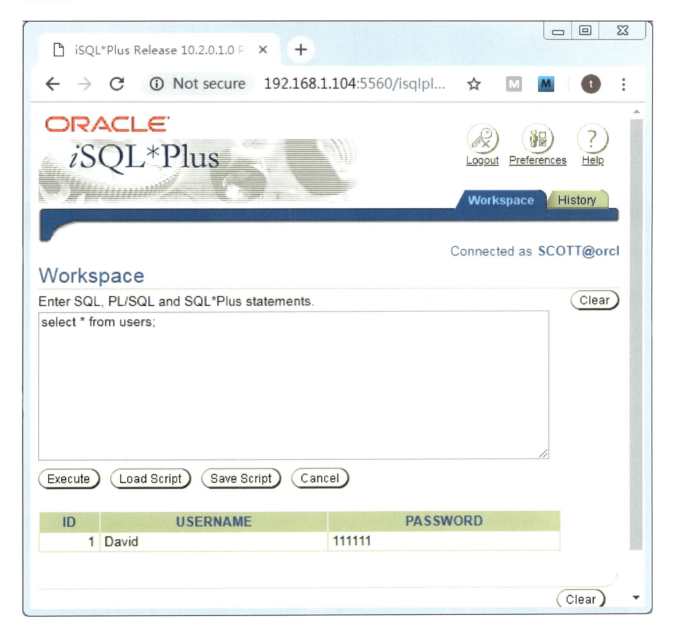

6. Add TestFind.java Read data from users table

```java
import java.sql.*;
public class TestFind {
   public static void main(String[] args) {
      Connection conn = null;
      try {
         Class.forName("oracle.jdbc.driver.OracleDriver");
         conn = DriverManager.getConnection("jdbc:oracle:thin:@192.168.1.104:1521:orcl",
"scott", "verejava1981");
         //sql read all data from table: users
         String sql = "select * from users";
         Statement stmt = conn.createStatement();

         ResultSet rs = stmt.executeQuery(sql); //all users store into ResultSet
         while (rs.next()) {
            int id = rs.getInt("id");
            String username = rs.getString("username");
            String password = rs.getString("password");
            System.out.println(id + "," + username + "," + password);
         }
      } catch (Exception e) {
         e.printStackTrace();
      } finally {
         try {
            conn.close();
         } catch (SQLException e) {
            e.printStackTrace();
         }
      }
   }
}
```

Result:

```
Problems  @ Javadoc  Declaration  Console 

<terminated> TestFind [Java Application] C:\Program Files (x86)\Java
1,David,111111
```

7. Add TestUpdate.java Update data to users table

```java
import java.sql.*;
public class TestUpdate {

    public static void main(String[] args) {
        Connection conn = null;
        try {
            Class.forName("oracle.jdbc.driver.OracleDriver");

            conn = DriverManager.getConnection("jdbc:oracle:thin:@192.168.1.104:1521:orcl",
"scott", "verejava1981");

            //sql statement update data to table: users
            String sql = "update users set password='222222' where id=1";

            Statement stmt = conn.createStatement();
            stmt.executeUpdate(sql);

        } catch (Exception e) {
            e.printStackTrace();
        } finally {
            try {
                conn.close();
            } catch (SQLException e) {
                e.printStackTrace();
            }
        }
    }
}
```

Result:

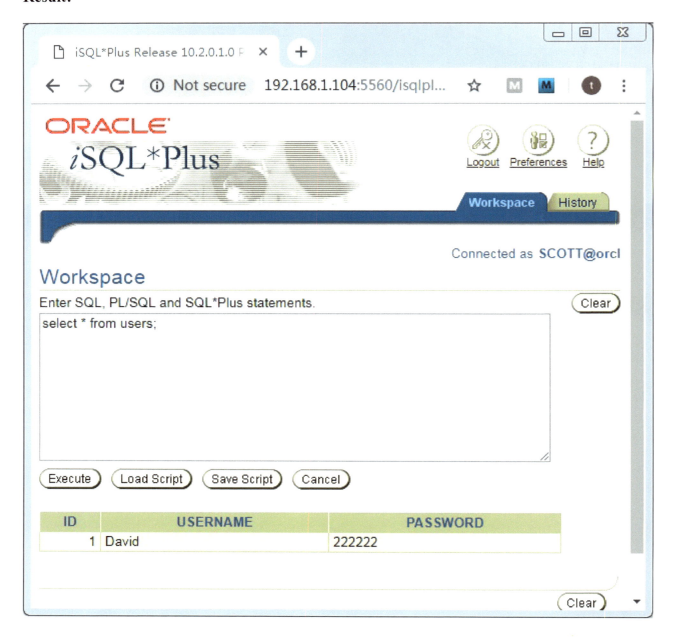

8. Add TestDelete.java **delete data from** users **table**

```java
import java.sql.*;
public class TestDelete {

    public static void main(String[] args) {
        Connection conn = null;
        try {
            Class.forName("oracle.jdbc.driver.OracleDriver");

            conn = DriverManager.getConnection("jdbc:oracle:thin:@192.168.1.104:1521:orcl",
"scott", "verejava1981");

            //sql statement delete data from table: users
            String sql = "delete from users where id=1";

            Statement stmt = conn.createStatement();
            stmt.executeUpdate(sql);
        } catch (Exception e) {
            e.printStackTrace();
        } finally {
            try {
                conn.close();
            } catch (SQLException e) {
                e.printStackTrace();
            }
        }
    }
}
```

Result:

JDBC Precompiled CRUD

JDBC precompilation mode is faster, because it will pre-compile sql into cache

1. Create a table : book in test database

```
create table book
(
    id numeric,
    title varchar2(100),
    price    numeric(10,2),
    birth timestamp,
    publish_date timestamp,
    update_date timestamp
);
```

Result:

2. Precompilation mode Add book record

```java
import java.sql.*;
import java.util.Date;
public class TestAdd {

    public static void main(String[] args) {
        Connection conn = null;
        try {
            Class.forName("oracle.jdbc.driver.OracleDriver");

            conn = DriverManager.getConnection("jdbc:oracle:thin:@192.168.1.104:1521:orcl",
"scott", "verejava1981");

            //Precompilation mode sql statement insert data to table: book
            String sql = "insert into
book(id,title,price,birth,publish_date,update_date)values(?,?,?,?,?,?)";

            PreparedStatement pstmt = conn.prepareStatement(sql);
            pstmt.setString(1, "1");
            pstmt.setString(2, "Easy Learning Java");
            pstmt.setFloat(3, 40.55f);
            pstmt.setTimestamp(4, new Timestamp(new Date().getTime()));
            pstmt.setTimestamp(5, new Timestamp(new Date().getTime()));
            pstmt.setTimestamp(6, new Timestamp(new Date().getTime()));

            pstmt.executeUpdate();

        } catch (Exception e) {
            e.printStackTrace();
        } finally {
            try {
                conn.close();
            } catch (SQLException e) {
                e.printStackTrace();
            }
        }
    }
}
```

Result:

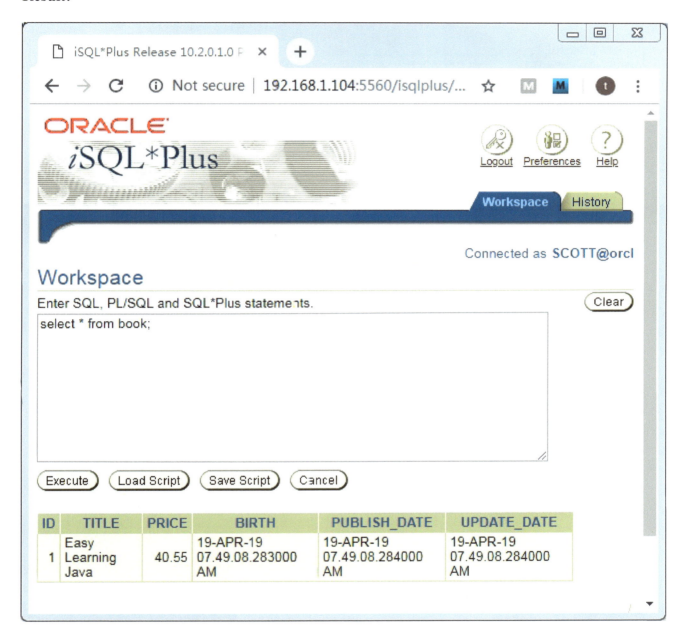

3. Precompilation mode Find the data of the book record id=1

```java
import java.sql.*;
public class TestFind {
    public static void main(String[] args) {
        Connection conn = null;
        try {
            Class.forName("oracle.jdbc.driver.OracleDriver");
            conn = DriverManager.getConnection("jdbc:oracle:thin:@192.168.1.104:1521:orcl", "scott", "verejava1981");
            //Precompilation mode sql statement query data from book
            String sql = "select * from book where id=?";
            PreparedStatement pstmt = conn.prepareStatement(sql);
            pstmt.setInt(1, 1);

            ResultSet rs = pstmt.executeQuery();
            while (rs.next()) {
                int id = rs.getInt("id");
                String title = rs.getString("title");
                float price = rs.getFloat("price");
                String birth = rs.getString("birth");
                Timestamp publish_date = rs.getTimestamp("publish_date");
                Timestamp update_date = rs.getTimestamp("update_date");
                System.out.println(id + "," + title + "," + price + "," + birth + "," + publish_date + "," + update_date);
            }
        } catch (Exception e) {
            e.printStackTrace();
        } finally {
            try {
                conn.close();
            } catch (SQLException e) {
                e.printStackTrace();
            }
        }
    }
}
```

Result:

1,Easy Learning Java,40.55,2019-4-19.7.49. 8. 283000000,2019-04-19 07:49:08.284,2019-04-19 07:49:08.284

4. Precompilation mode Modify the book record id=1

```java
import java.sql.*;
import java.util.Date;
public class TestUpdate {
    public static void main(String[] args) {

        Connection conn = null;
        try {
            Class.forName("oracle.jdbc.driver.OracleDriver");

            conn = DriverManager.getConnection("jdbc:oracle:thin:@192.168.1.104:1521:orcl",
"scott", "verejava1981");

            //Precompilation mode sql statement update data into book
            String sql = "update book set title=?,price=?,birth=?,publish_date=?,update_date=?
where id=?";
            PreparedStatement pstmt = conn.prepareStatement(sql);
            pstmt.setString(1, "Life is not limited");
            pstmt.setFloat(2, 50.55f);
            pstmt.setDate(3, new java.sql.Date(new Date().getTime()));
            pstmt.setTimestamp(4, new Timestamp(new Date().getTime()));
            pstmt.setTimestamp(5, new Timestamp(new Date().getTime()));
            pstmt.setInt(6, 1);

            pstmt.executeUpdate();

        } catch (Exception e) {
            e.printStackTrace();
        } finally {
            try {
                conn.close();
            } catch (SQLException e) {
                e.printStackTrace();
            }
        }
    }
}
```

Result:

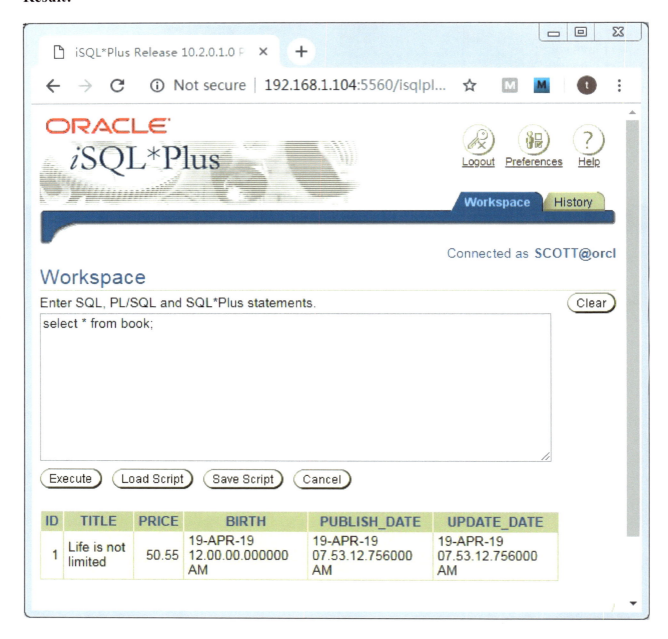

5. Precompilation mode Delete the book record id=1

```java
import java.sql.*;
import java.util.Date;
public class TestDelete {

  public static void main(String[] args) {

    Connection conn = null;
    try {
      Class.forName("oracle.jdbc.driver.OracleDriver");

      conn = DriverManager.getConnection("jdbc:oracle:thin:@192.168.1.104:1521:orcl",
"scott", "verejava1981");

      //Precompilation mode sql statement delete data from book
      String sql = "delete from book where id=?";
      PreparedStatement pstmt = conn.prepareStatement(sql);
      pstmt.setInt(1, 1);

      pstmt.executeUpdate();

    } catch (Exception e) {
      e.printStackTrace();
    } finally {
      try {
        conn.close();
      } catch (SQLException e) {
        e.printStackTrace();
      }
    }
  }
}
```

Result:

JDBC Tool DBUtil

```
                    DBUtil

  DBUtil()
  openConnection() : Connection
  executeUpdate(sql : String) : boolean
  executeQuery(scl : String) : ResultSet
  executeUpdate(sql : String, params : Object[]) : boolean
  executeQuery(sql : String, params : Object[]) : ResultSet
  DBClose()
```

```java
import java.sql.*;
import java.util.Date;

public class DBUtil {

    protected Connection conn;
    protected Statement stmt;

    public DBUtil() {
        try {
            Class.forName("oracle.jdbc.driver.OracleDriver");
        } catch (ClassNotFoundException e) {
            e.printStackTrace();
        }
    }

    //Open JDBC Database Connection
    public Connection openConnection() {
        try {
            return DriverManager.getConnection("jdbc:oracle:thin:@192.168.1.104:1521:orcl",
"scott", "verejava1981");
        } catch (SQLException e) {
            e.printStackTrace();
        }
        return null;
    }
}
```

```java
//execute add delete update sql
public boolean executeUpdate(String sql) {
   conn = openConnection();

   try {
      Statement stmt = conn.createStatement();
      if (stmt.executeUpdate(sql) > 0) {
         return true;
      }
   } catch (SQLException e) {
      e.printStackTrace();
   } finally {
      if (conn != null) {
         try {
            conn.close();
         } catch (SQLException e) {
            e.printStackTrace();
         }
      }
   }
   return false;
}

//execute query sql
public ResultSet executeQuery(String sql) {
   conn = openConnection();
   try {
      Statement stmt = conn.createStatement();
      return stmt.executeQuery(sql);
   } catch (SQLException e) {
      e.printStackTrace();
   }
   return null;
}
```

```java
//Precompilation Add Delete Update
public boolean executeUpdate(String sql, Object[] params) {
    conn = openConnection();
    try {
        PreparedStatement pstmt = conn.prepareStatement(sql);
        for (int i = 0; params != null && i < params.length; i++) {
            Object param = params[i];
            if (param instanceof Integer) {
                pstmt.setInt(i + 1, Integer.parseInt(param.toString()));
            }
            if (param instanceof Float) {
                pstmt.setFloat(i + 1, Float.parseFloat(param.toString()));
            }
            if (param instanceof Double) {
                pstmt.setDouble(i + 1, Double.parseDouble(param.toString()));
            }
            if (param instanceof String) {
                pstmt.setString(i + 1, param.toString());
            }
            if (param instanceof Date) {
                java.util.Date date = (java.util.Date) param;
                pstmt.setTimestamp(i + 1, new Timestamp(date.getTime()));
            }
        }
        if (pstmt.executeUpdate() > 0) {
            return true;
        }
    } catch (SQLException e) {
        e.printStackTrace();
    } finally {
        DBClose();
    }
    return false;
}
```

```java
//select * from book where id=? and title=?;
public ResultSet executeQuery(String sql, Object[] params) {
    conn = openConnection();
    try {
        PreparedStatement pstmt = conn.prepareStatement(sql);
        for (int i = 0; params != null && i < params.length; i++) {
            Object param = params[i];
            if (param instanceof Integer) {
                pstmt.setInt(i + 1, Integer.parseInt(param.toString()));
            }
            if (param instanceof Float) {
                pstmt.setFloat(i + 1, Float.parseFloat(param.toString()));
            }
            if (param instanceof Double) {
                pstmt.setDouble(i + 1, Double.parseDouble(param.toString()));
            }
            if (param instanceof String) {
                pstmt.setString(i + 1, param.toString());
            }
            if (param instanceof Date) {
                java.util.Date date = (java.util.Date) param;
                pstmt.setTimestamp(i + 1, new Timestamp(date.getTime()));
            }
        }
        return pstmt.executeQuery();
    } catch (SQLException e) {
        e.printStackTrace();
    }
    return null;
}

//close database connection
public void DBClose() {
    if (conn != null) {
        try {
            conn.close();
        } catch (SQLException e) {
            e.printStackTrace();
        }
    }
}
}
```

DBUtil User CRUD

1. Create a model class: User mapping table : users

```java
public class User {
    private int id;
    private String username;
    private String password;

    public int getId() {
        return id;
    }

    public void setId(int id) {
        this.id = id;
    }

    public String getUsername() {
        return username;
    }

    public void setUsername(String username) {
        this.username = username;
    }

    public String getPassword() {
        return password;
    }

    public void setPassword(String password) {
        this.password = password;
    }

}
```

2. DBUtil adds the User to the users table

```java
public class TestAdd {

    public static void main(String[] args) {

        DBUtil db = new DBUtil();

        User user = new User();
        user.setId(2);
        user.setUsername("Grace");
        user.setPassword("444444");

        String sql = "insert into users(id,username,password)values("+user.getId()+",'" +
user.getUsername() + "','" + user.getPassword() + "')";

        db.executeUpdate(sql);
    }
}
```

Result:

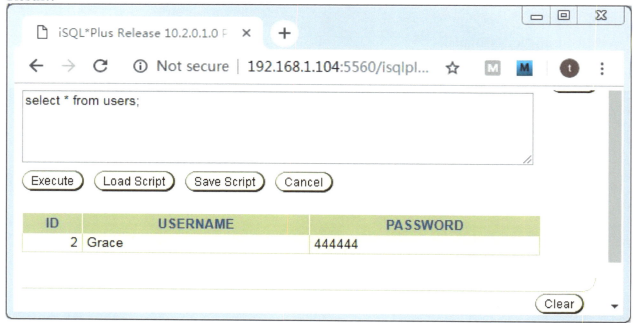

3. DBUtil reads the data of the users table with id=2 and stores it in the User.

```java
import java.sql.*;
public class TestFindOne {

    public static void main(String[] args) {

        DBUtil db = new DBUtil();
        String sql = "select * from users where id=2 ";
        ResultSet rs = db.executeQuery(sql);

        User user = null;
        try {
            if (rs.next()) {
                user = new User();
                user.setId(rs.getInt("id"));
                user.setUsername(rs.getString("username"));
                user.setPassword(rs.getString("password"));
            }
        } catch (SQLException e) {
            e.printStackTrace();
        } finally {
            db.DBClose();
        }

        if (user != null) {
            System.out.println(user.getId() + "," + user.getUsername() + "," + user.getPassword());
        }
    }
}
```

Result:

Problems @ Javadoc Declaration Console

<terminated> TestFindOne [Java Application] C:\Program Files (x86)\

2,Grace,444444

27

4. DBUtil update the data of the users table id=2

```java
public class TestUpdate {

public static void main(String[] args) {

    DBUtil db = new DBUtil();

    User user = new User();
    user.setId(2);

    String sql = "update users set password='555555' where id=" + user.getId();
    db.executeUpdate(sql);
  }
}
```

Result:

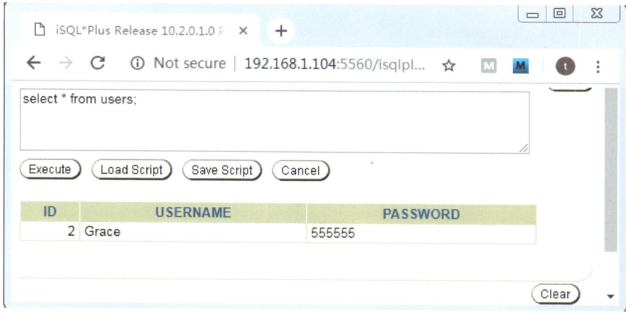

5. **DBUtil** deletes the data of the **users** table id=2

```java
public class TestDelete {

    public static void main(String[] args) {

        DBUtil db = new DBUtil();

        User user = new User();
        user.setId(2);

        String sql = "delete from users where id=" + user.getId();
        db.executeUpdate(sql);

    }
}
```

Result:

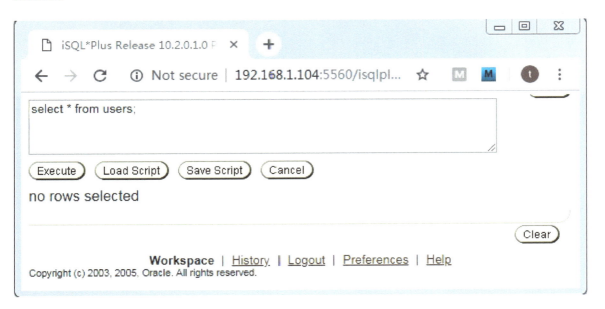

6. DBUtil reads multiple data of users and stores it in List<User>

Insert 2 items data into table : users;

insert into users(id,username,password)values(3,'James','666666');

insert into users(id,username,password)values(4,'Isacc','777777');

commit;

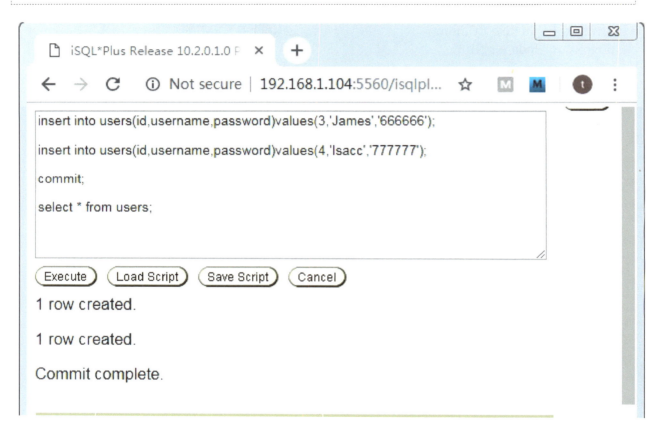

Create TestFind.java

```java
import java.sql.*;
import java.util.*;
public class TestFind {
  public static void main(String[] args) {
    DBUtil db = new DBUtil();
    String sql = "select * from users";
    ResultSet rs = db.executeQuery(sql);

    List<User> userList = new ArrayList<User>();
    try {
      while (rs.next()) {
        User user = new User();
        user.setId(rs.getInt("id"));
        user.setUsername(rs.getString("username"));
        user.setPassword(rs.getString("password"));
        userList.add(user);
      }
    } catch (SQLException e) {
      e.printStackTrace();
    } finally {
      db.DBClose();
    }

    for (int i = 0; i < userList.size(); i++) {
      User user = userList.get(i);
      System.out.println(user.getId() + "," + user.getUsername() + "," + user.getPassword());
    }
  }
}
```

Result:

```
Problems  @ Javadoc  Declaration  Console ⊠
<terminated> TestFind (2) [Java Application] C:\Program Files (x86)\J
3,James,666666
4,Isacc,777777
```

31

DBUtil UserDAO CRUD

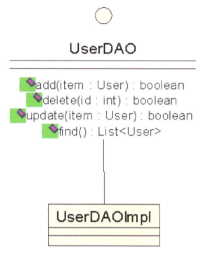

1. Create a data access interface: UserDAO

```java
import java.util.*;

public interface UserDAO {

    public boolean add(User item);

    public boolean delete(int id);

    public boolean update(User item);

    public List<User> find();
}
```

2. Data access implementation class : UserDAOImpl

```java
import java.sql.*;
import java.util.*;

public class UserDAOImpl implements UserDAO {

    private DBUtil db;

    public UserDAOImpl() {
        db = new DBUtil();
    }

    @Override
    public boolean add(User item) {
        String sql = "insert into users(id,username,password)values(?,?,?)";
        Object[] params={item.getId(),item.getUsername(),item.getPassword()};

        return db.executeUpdate(sql, params);
    }

    @Override
    public boolean delete(int id) {
        String sql = "delete from users where id=" + id;
        return db.executeUpdate(sql);
    }

    @Override
    public boolean update(User item) {
        String sql = "update users set username=?,password=? where id =?" ;
        Object[] params={item.getUsername(),item.getPassword(),item.getId()};

        return db.executeUpdate(sql, params);
    }
```

```java
@Override
public List<User> find() {
    List<User> userList = new ArrayList<User> ();
    String sql = "select * from users";
    ResultSet rs = db.executeQuery(sql);
    try {
        while (rs.next()) {
            int id = rs.getInt("id");
            String username = rs.getString("username");
            String password = rs.getString("password");
            userList.add(new User(id, username, password));
        }
    } catch (SQLException e) {
        e.printStackTrace();
    } finally {
        db.DBClose();
    }
    return userList;
}
}
```

3. UserDAO TestAdd

```java
public class TestAdd {

  public static void main(String[] args) {

    UserDAO userDAO = new UserDAOImpl();
    userDAO.add(new User(5,"Sala", "888888"));

  }
}
```

Result:

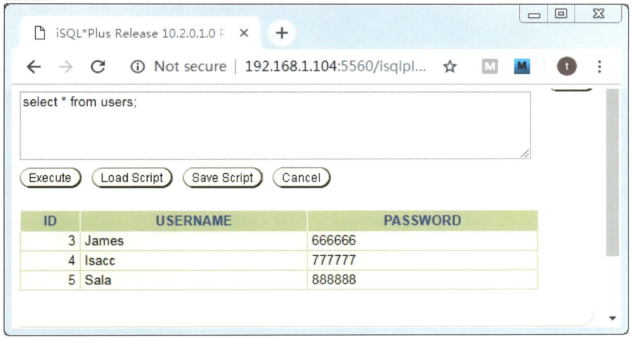

4. UserDAO TestFind

```java
import java.util.*;

public class TestFind {

    public static void main(String[] args) {

        UserDAO userDAO = new UserDAOImpl();
        List<User> userList = userDAO.find();

        for (User item : userList) {
            System.out.println(item.getId() + "," + item.getUsername() + "," +
item.getPassword());
        }
    }
}
```

Result:

```
 Problems  @ Javadoc  Declaration  Console ⊠        ▭ ☐
                   ■ ✖ ✖ | ☰ ☰ 🗗 🗗 | 🗗 🖳 ▾ 🗗 ▾
<terminated> TestFind (3) [Java Application] C:\Program Files (x86)\J
3,James,666666                                              ▲
4,Isacc,777777
5,Sala,888888
                                                            ▾
 ◄                                                    ►
```

5. UserDAO TestUpdate

```java
public class TestUpdate {

    public static void main(String[] args) {

        UserDAO userDAO = new UserDAOImpl();
        userDAO.update(new User(5, "Sala", "999999"));
    }
}
```

Result:

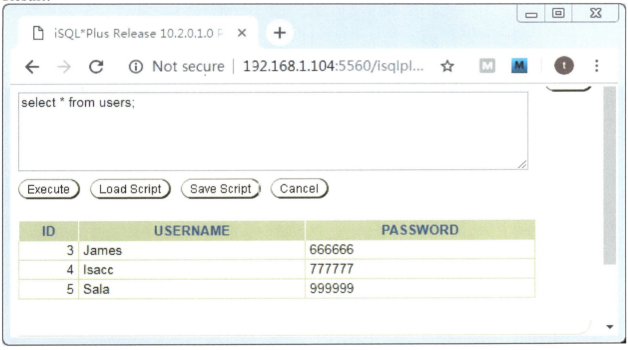

6. UserDAO TestDelete

```java
public class TestDelete {

  public static void main(String[] args) {

    UserDAO userDAO = new UserDAOImpl();
    userDAO.delete(5);
  }
}
```

Result:

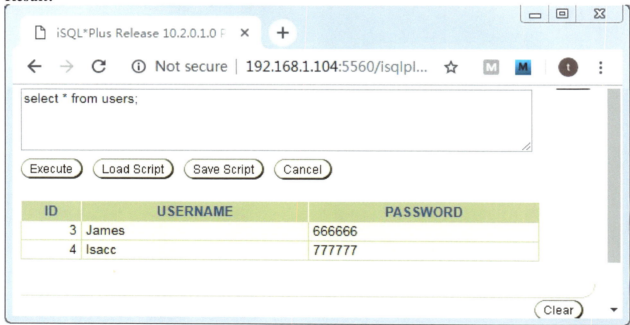

DBUtil UserDAO Paging Query

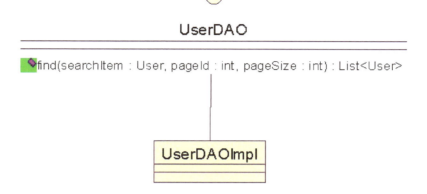

1. Create a data access interface: UserDAO

```
import java.util.*;

public interface UserDAO {

    public List<User> find(User searchItem,int pageId,int pageSize);

}
```

2. Data access implementation class : UserDAOImpl

```java
import java.sql.*;
import java.util.*;
public class UserDAOImpl implements UserDAO {
    private DBUtil db;
    public UserDAOImpl() {
        db = new DBUtil();
    }

    public List<User> find(User searchItem, int pageId, int pageSize) {
        ResultSet rs = null;
        List<User> userList = new ArrayList<User>();
        try {
            boolean b = false;
            StringBuffer where = new StringBuffer();
            String fvalue = null;
            fvalue = searchItem.getUsername();
            if (fvalue != null && fvalue.length() > 0) {
                if (b)
                    where.append(" and");
                where.append("  username like '%" + fvalue + "%'");
                b = true;
            }
            if (!where.toString().equals(""))
                where.insert(0, " where ");

            String sql = "SELECT * FROM (SELECT ROWNUM rn,temp_users.* FROM
(SELECT * FROM users ORDER BY id ASC) temp_users) WHERE rn>" + (pageId - 1) *
pageSize + " AND rn <=" + pageId * pageSize ;
            rs = db.executeQuery(sql);
            while (rs.next()) {
                int id = rs.getInt("id");
                String username = rs.getString("username");
                String password = rs.getString("password");
                userList.add(new User(id, username, password));
            }
        } catch (SQLException e) {
            e.printStackTrace();
        } finally {
            db.DBClose();
        }
        return userList;
    }
}
```

3. Insert test data into table : users

```
insert into users(id,username,password)values(6,'David','111111');
insert into users(id,username,password)values(7,'Sala','222222');
insert into users(id,username,password)values(8,'Mathew','333333');
insert into users(id,username,password)values(9,'Luka','4444444');
insert into users(id,username,password)values(10,'John','555555');
commit;
```

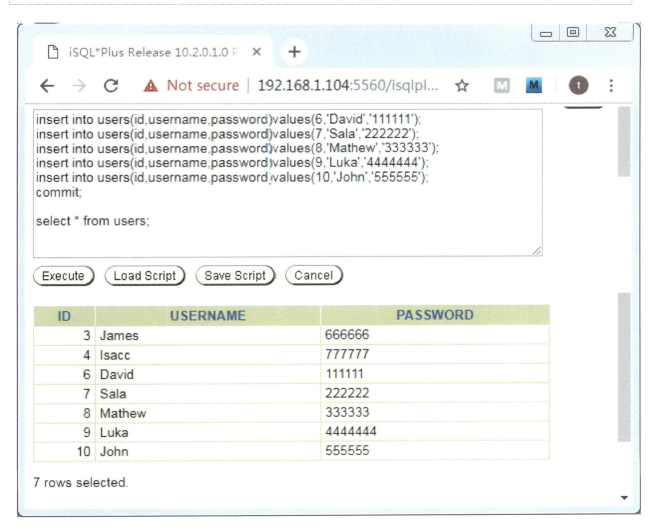

4. Get the first page data from : users

```java
import java.text.SimpleDateFormat;
import java.util.*;

public class TestFind {

    public static void main(String[] args) {
        int pageId = 1; //Current page
        int pageSize = 3; //Number of records per page
        User searchItem = new User();
        searchItem.setUsername("");

        UserDAO userDAO = new UserDAOImpl();
        List<User> userList = userDAO.find(searchItem, pageId, pageSize);
        for (User item : userList) {
            System.out.println(item.getId() + "," + item. getUsername() + "," +
item.getPassword());
        }
    }
}
```

Result:

```
Problems  @ Javadoc  Declaration  Console

3,James,666666
4,Isacc,777777
6,David,111111
```

5. change int pageId = 2; Get the second page data from : users

```
Problems  @ Javadoc  Declaration  Console

7,Sala,222222
8,Mathew,333333
9,Luka,4444444
```

JDBC Reflections Any Object

1. Create a class: Session Save any Object by reflection

```java
import java.lang.reflect.*;
import java.util.*;

public class Session {

    private DBUtil db;

    public Session() {
        db = new DBUtil();
    }

    public boolean save(Object obj,String tableName) {
        Class clazz = obj.getClass();
        String className = clazz.getName(); //Get the full class name

        try {
            clazz = Class.forName(className);

            //Get the properties of any model class as the column name of the table
            Field[] fields = clazz.getDeclaredFields();

            //Get the built insert sql statement
            Object[] returnObj = buildInsertSQL(fields, obj, tableName);
            String sql = returnObj[0].toString();
            Object[] params = (Object[]) returnObj[1];

            return db.executeUpdate(sql, params);

        } catch (Exception e) {
            e.printStackTrace();

        } finally {
            db.DBClose();
        }
        return false;
    }
}
```

```java
//Get the built insert sql statement
private Object[] buildInsertSQL(Field[] fields, Object obj, String tableName) {
    Object[] returnObj = new Object[2];
    Class clazz = obj.getClass();

    List<Object> params = new ArrayList<Object>();

    StringBuffer sb = new StringBuffer();
    StringBuffer sbValue = new StringBuffer();

    sb.append("insert into ").append(tableName).append("(");

    for (int i = 0; i < fields.length; i++) {
        Field field = fields[i];
        String fieldName = field.getName();

        sb.append(fieldName).append(",");
        sbValue.append("?,");

        String firstFieldName = fieldName.substring(0, 1).toUpperCase();
        String leftFieldName = fieldName.substring(1);
        String methodName = "get" + firstFieldName + leftFieldName;

        Method method;
        try {
            method = clazz.getDeclaredMethod(methodName, new Class[] {});
            Object resultObj = method.invoke(obj, new Object[] {});
            params.add(resultObj);
        } catch (Exception e) {
            e.printStackTrace();
        }
    }
    sb.delete(sb.length() - 1, sb.length());
    sb.append(")values(");
    sbValue.delete(sbValue.length() - 1, sbValue.length());
    sb.append(sbValue).append(")");

    returnObj[0] = sb.toString();
    returnObj[1] = params.toArray();
    return returnObj;
  }
}
```

2. Create Testing class: TestSessionAdd.java

```java
public class TestSessionAdd {
public static void main(String[] args) {

    Session session=new Session();

    User user=new User(11,"Ablahan","888888");
    session.save(user,"users");

    User user2=new User(12,"Make","999999");
    session.save(user2,"users");

    User user3=new User(13,"Lebeka","101010");
    session.save(user3,"users");


  }
}
```

Result:

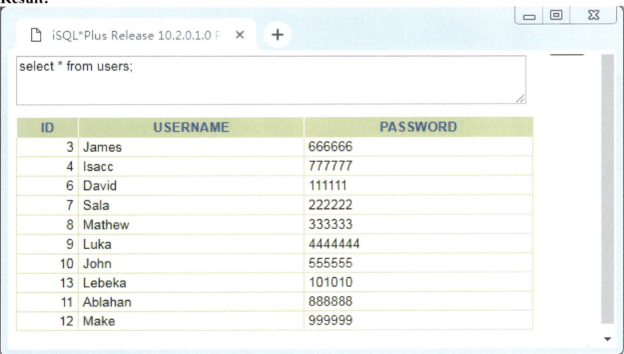

ID	USERNAME	PASSWORD
3	James	666666
4	Isacc	777777
6	David	111111
7	Sala	222222
8	Mathew	333333
9	Luka	4444444
10	John	555555
13	Lebeka	101010
11	Ablahan	888888
12	Make	999999

JDBC Transaction

Transaction: All SQL commits successfully, or all rollback fails

1. 10 data are inserted in bulk

```java
import java.sql.*;
import java.util.Date;
public class TestTransaction {
   public static void main(String[] args) {
      DBUtil db = new DBUtil();
      Connection conn = db.openConnection();
      try {
         conn.setAutoCommit(false);//Set to manually submit
         for (int i = 0; i < 10; i++) {
            String sql = "insert into
book(id,title,price,birth,publish_date,update_date)values(?,?,?,?,?,?)";

            PreparedStatement pstmt = conn.prepareStatement(sql);
            pstmt.setInt(1, i+2);
            pstmt.setString(2, "Motivating books " + i);
            pstmt.setFloat(3, 40.55f + 1);
            pstmt.setTimestamp(4, new Timestamp(new Date().getTime()));
            pstmt.setTimestamp(5, new Timestamp(new Date().getTime()));
            pstmt.setTimestamp(6, new Timestamp(new Date().getTime()));

            pstmt.executeUpdate();
            conn.commit();// 10 data inserted, batch submit
         }
      } catch (SQLException e) {
         try {
            conn.rollback();//10 pieces of data rollback failed
         } catch (SQLException e1) {
            e1.printStackTrace();
         }
         e.printStackTrace();
      } finally {
         db.DBClose();
      }
   }
}
```

Result:

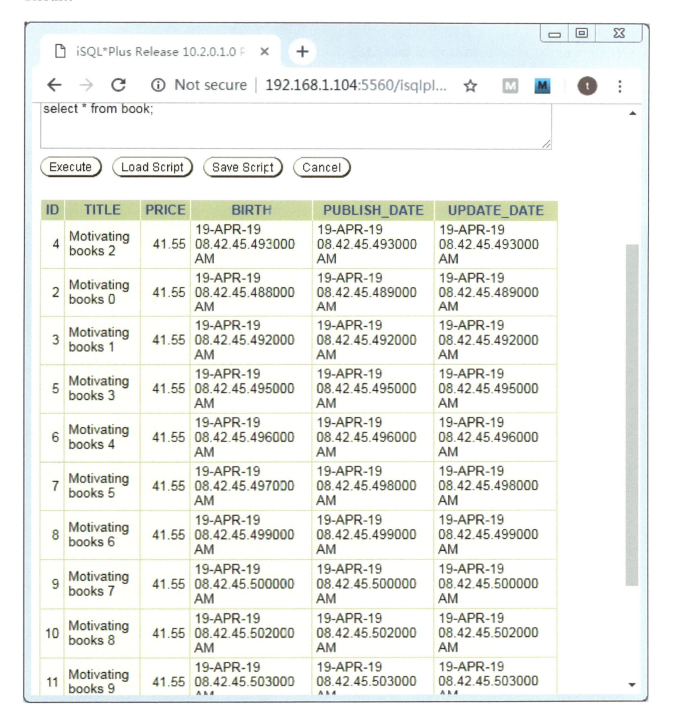

JDBC Save and Export Text File

1. Create a table: textfile to store a text file

```
create table textfile
(
    id numeric,
    content clob
);
```

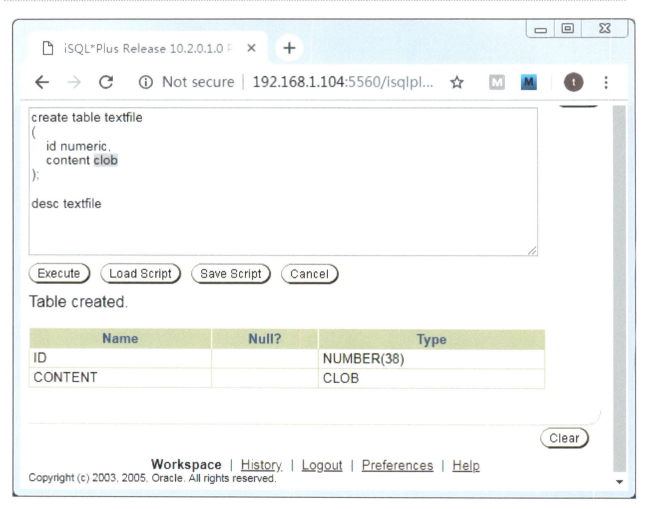

2. Create a text file: text.txt content below

Having a specific meaning and purpose in your life helps to encourage you towards living a fulfilling and inspired life.

My friends, love is better than anger. Hope is better than fear. Optimism is better than despair. So let us be loving, hopeful and optimistic. And we'll change the world.

3. Save the text.txt to the content field of the table: textfile

```java
import java.io.*;
import java.sql.*;

public class TestAdd {

    public static void main(String[] args) {

        DBUtil db = new DBUtil();
        Connection conn = db.openConnection();
        String sql = "insert into textfile(id,content)values(?,?)";

        try {
            PreparedStatement pstmt = conn.prepareStatement(sql);
            File file = new File("C:/Users/tim/Desktop/text.txt");
            Reader reader = new FileReader(file);
            pstmt.setInt(1, 1);
            pstmt.setCharacterStream(2, reader, (int)file.length());

            pstmt.executeUpdate();
        } catch (Exception e) {
            e.printStackTrace();
        } finally {
            db.DBClose();
        }
    }
}
```

Result:

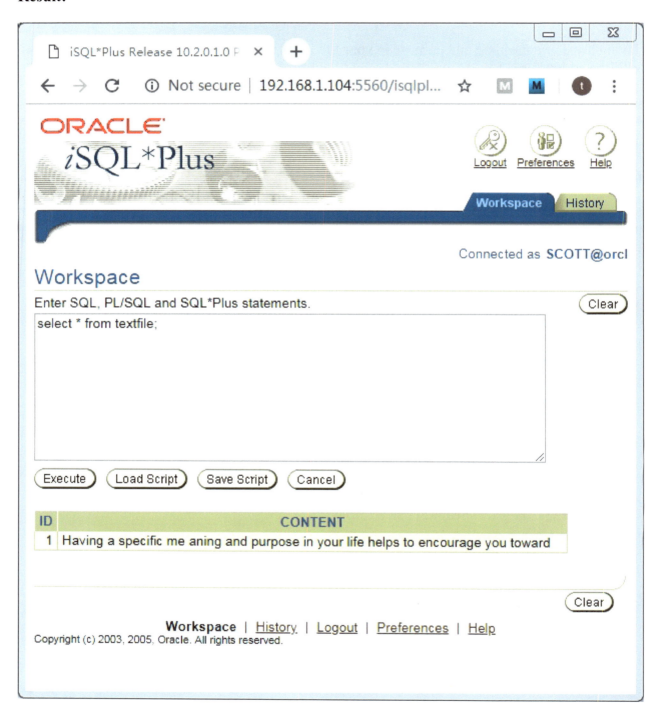

4. Read content field of the table: textfile to store in text2.txt

```java
import java.io.*;
import java.sql.*;
public class TestFind {

    public static void main(String[] args) {
        DBUtil db = new DBUtil();
        Connection conn = db.openConnection();
        String sql = "select * from textfile where id=1";

        try {
            PreparedStatement pstmt = conn.prepareStatement(sql);
            ResultSet rs = pstmt.executeQuery(sql);

            StringBuilder sb = new StringBuilder();
            if (rs.next()) {
                Reader reader = rs.getCharacterStream("content");
                int l = 0;
                char[] cbuf = new char[1024];
                while ((l = reader.read(cbuf)) != -1) {
                    sb.append(new String(cbuf, 0, l));
                }
            }

            //Save the read data to test2.txt
            Writer writer = new FileWriter(new File("C:/Users/tim/Desktop/test2.txt"));
            writer.write(sb.toString());
            writer.flush();
            writer.close();
        } catch (Exception e) {
            e.printStackTrace();
        } finally {
            db.DBClose();
        }
    }
}
```

Result:

test2.txt

Having a specific meaning and purpose in your life helps to encourage you towards living a fulfilling and inspired life.

My friends, love is better than anger. Hope is better than fear. Optimism is better than despair. So let us be loving, hopeful and optimistic. And we'll change the world.

JDBC Save and Export Picture

1. Create a table: binaryfile to store a picture

```
create table binaryfile
(
    id numeric,
    picture blob
);
```

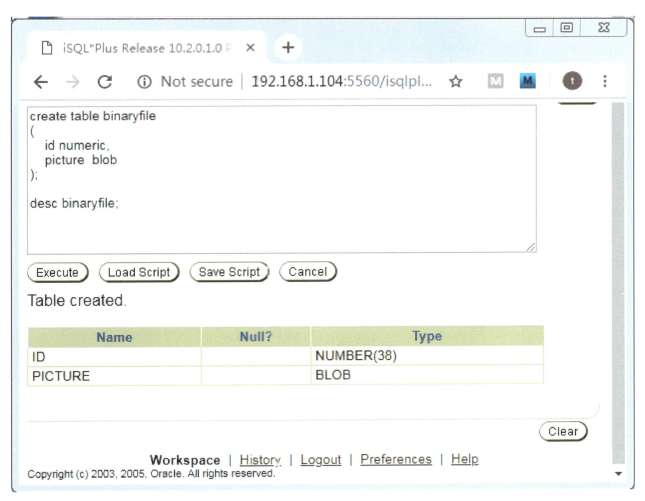

2. Save the java.jpg to the file field of the table: binaryfile

```java
import java.io.*;
import java.sql.*;

public class TestAdd {

    public static void main(String[] args) {

        DBUtil db = new DBUtil();
        Connection conn = db.openConnection();
        String sql = "insert into binaryfile(id,picture)values(?,?)";

        try {
            PreparedStatement pstmt = conn.prepareStatement(sql);
            File file = new File("C:/Users/tim/Desktop/java.jpg");
            InputStream inputStream = new FileInputStream(file);
            pstmt.setInt(1,1);
            pstmt.setBlob(2, inputStream, (int)file.length());

            pstmt.executeUpdate();
        } catch (Exception e) {
            e.printStackTrace();
        } finally {
            db.DBClose();
        }
    }
}
```

4. Read file field of the table: binaryfile to store in java2.jpg

```java
import java.io.*;
import java.sql.*;

public class TestFind {

  public static void main(String[] args) {

    DBUtil db = new DBUtil();
    Connection conn = db.openConnection();
    String sql = "select * from binaryfile where id=1";

    OutputStream os = null;
    try {
      PreparedStatement pstmt = conn.prepareStatement(sql);
      ResultSet rs = pstmt.executeQuery();
      os = new FileOutputStream("C:/Users/tim/Desktop/java2.jpg");
      while (rs.next()) {
        Blob blob = rs.getBlob("picture");
        InputStream is = blob.getBinaryStream();
        int l = 0;
        byte[] data = new byte[1024];
        while ((l = is.read(data)) != -1) {
          os.write(data, 0, l);
        }
        os.flush();
      }
    } catch (Exception e) {
      e.printStackTrace();
    } finally {
      try {
        os.close();
      } catch (IOException e) {
        e.printStackTrace();
      }
      db.DBClose();
    }
  }
}
```

Result:

JDBC Call Stored Procedure Add User

1. Create a stored procedure: sp_user_add in Oracle

```
create or replace procedure sp_user_add(in_id in users.id%TYPE,in_username in
users.username%TYPE,in_password in users.password%TYPE)
as

begin
  insert into users(id,username,password)values(in_id,in_username,in_password);
end;
```

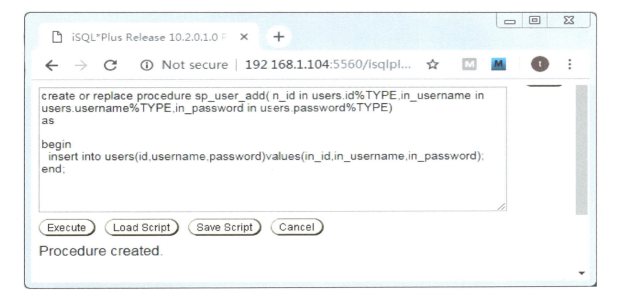

2. Calling a stored procedure : sp_user_add

```java
import java.sql.*;
public class TestAdd {
    public static void main(String[] args) {
        DBUtil db = new DBUtil();
        Connection conn = db.openConnection();
        String sql = "call sp_user_add(?,?,?)";
        try {
            CallableStatement callStmt = conn.prepareCall(sql);
            callStmt.setInt(1,14);
            callStmt.setString(2, "Solomen");
            callStmt.setString(3, "202020");
            callStmt.executeUpdate();
        } catch (SQLException e) {
            e.printStackTrace();
        } finally {
            db.DBClose();
        }
    }
}
```

Result:

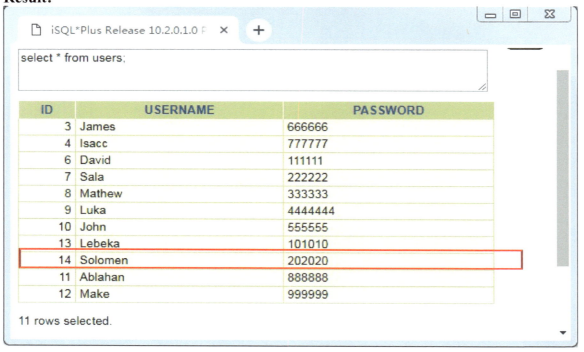

select * from users;

ID	USERNAME	PASSWORD
3	James	666666
4	Isacc	777777
6	David	111111
7	Sala	222222
8	Mathew	333333
9	Luka	4444444
10	John	555555
13	Lebeka	101010
14	Solomen	202020
11	Ablahan	888888
12	Make	999999

11 rows selected.

JDBC Call Stored Procedure Update User

1. Create a stored procedure: sp_user_update **in Oracle**

```
create or replace procedure sp_user_update(in_id  in users.id%TYPE,in_username in
users.username%TYPE,in_password in users.password%TYPE)
as

begin
  update users set username=in_username,password=in_password where id=in_id;
end;
```

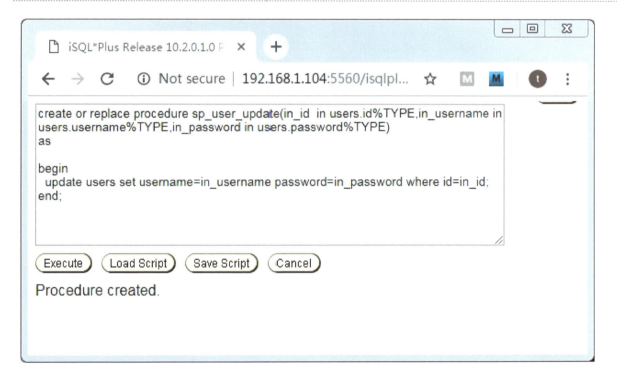

2. Calling a stored procedure : sp_user_update

```java
import java.sql.*;
public class TestUpdate {
    public static void main(String[] args) {
        DBUtil db = new DBUtil();
        Connection conn = db.openConnection();
        String sql = "call sp_user_update(?,?,?)";
        try {
            CallableStatement callStmt = conn.prepareCall(sql);
            callStmt.setInt(1, 14);
            callStmt.setString(2, "Solomen");
            callStmt.setString(3, "303030");
            callStmt.executeUpdate();
        } catch (SQLException e) {
            e.printStackTrace();
        } finally {
            db.DBClose();
        }
    }
}
```

Result:

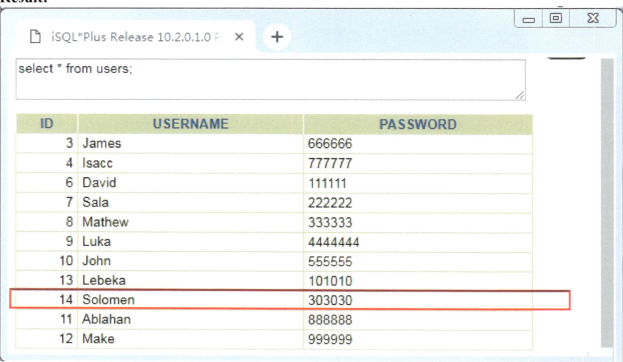

JDBC Call Stored Procedure Delete User

1. Create a stored procedure: sp_user_delete in Oracle

```
create or replace procedure sp_user_delete(in_id in users.id%TYPE)
as

begin
  delete from users where id=in_id;
end;
```

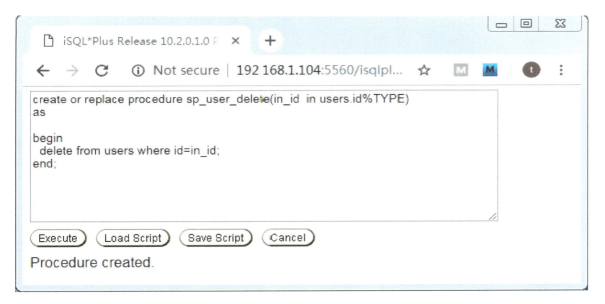

2. Calling a stored procedure : sp_user_delete

```java
import java.sql.*;
public class TestDelete {
   public static void main(String[] args) {
      DBUtil db = new DBUtil();
      Connection conn = db.openConnection();
      String sql = "call sp_user_delete(?)";
      try {
         CallableStatement callStmt = conn.prepareCall(sql);
         callStmt.setInt(1, 14);

         callStmt.executeUpdate();
      } catch (SQLException e) {
         e.printStackTrace();
      } finally {
         db.DBClose();
      }
   }
}
```

Result:

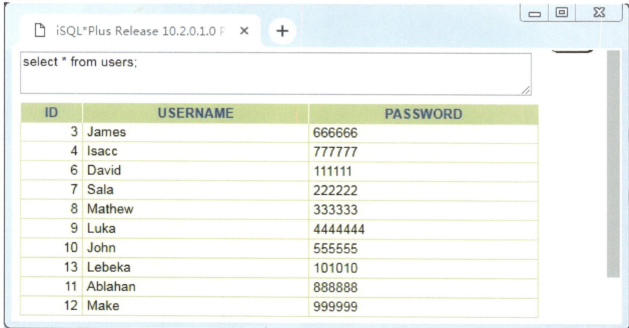

iSQL*Plus Release 10.2.0.1.0 F

select * from users;

ID	USERNAME	PASSWORD
3	James	666666
4	Isacc	777777
6	David	111111
7	Sala	222222
8	Mathew	333333
9	Luka	4444444
10	John	555555
13	Lebeka	101010
11	Ablahan	888888
12	Make	999999

JDBC Call Stored Procedure Query User

1. Create a package: MYPACKAGE in Oracle

CREATE OR REPLACE PACKAGE MYPACKAGE   **AS**

TYPE MY_CURSOR **IS REF CURSOR;**

END MYPACKAGE**;**

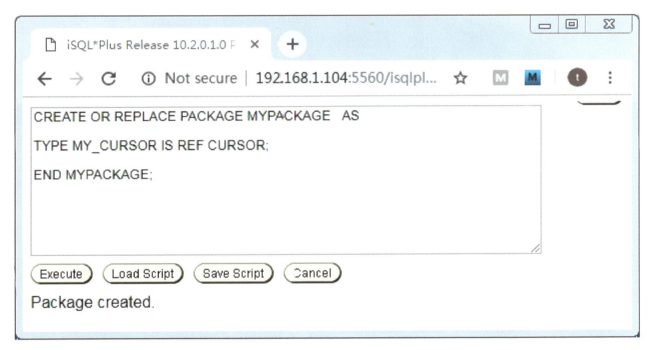

2. Create a stored procedure: sp_user_find in Oracle

```
CREATE OR REPLACE PROCEDURE sp_user_find(p_CURSOR out
MYPACKAGE.MY_CURSOR) IS

begin
  OPEN p_CURSOR FOR select * from users;
end;
```

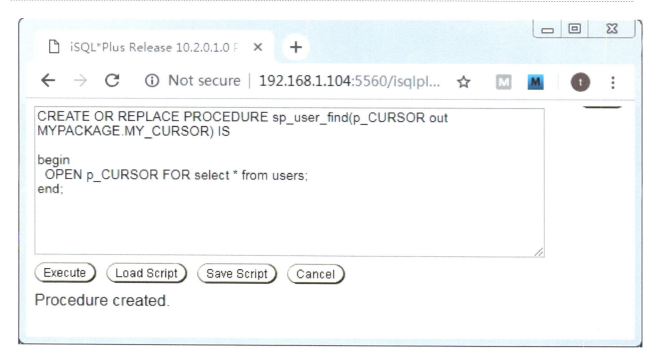

2. Calling a stored procedure : sp_user_find

```java
import java.sql.*;
public class TestFind {
  public static void main(String[] args) {
    DBUtil db = new DBUtil();
    Connection conn = db.openConnection();
    String sql = "call sp_user_find(?)";
    try {
      CallableStatement callStmt = conn.prepareCall(sql);
      callStmt.registerOutParameter(1, oracle.jdbc.OracleTypes.CURSOR);
      callStmt.execute();
      ResultSet rs = (ResultSet) callStmt.getObject(1);
      while (rs.next()) {
        int id = rs.getInt("id");
        String username = rs.getString("username");
        String password = rs.getString("password");
        System.out.println(id + "," + username + "," + password);
      }
    } catch (SQLException e) {
      e.printStackTrace();
    }
  }
}
```

Result:

Problems @ Javadoc Declaration Console

\<terminated\> TestFind (7) [Java Application] C:\Program Files (x86)\Java

```
3,James,666666
4,Isacc,777777
6,David,111111
7,Sala,222222
8,Mathew,333333
9,Luka,4444444
10,John,555555
11,Ablahan,888888
12,Make,999999
13,Lebeka,101010
```

JDBC Call Stored Procedure Return Parameter

1. Create a Add users and return the latest insert id: sp_user_count in Oracle

```
create or replace procedure sp_user_count(out_result out numeric)
as

begin
  select count(*) into out_result from users ;
end;
```

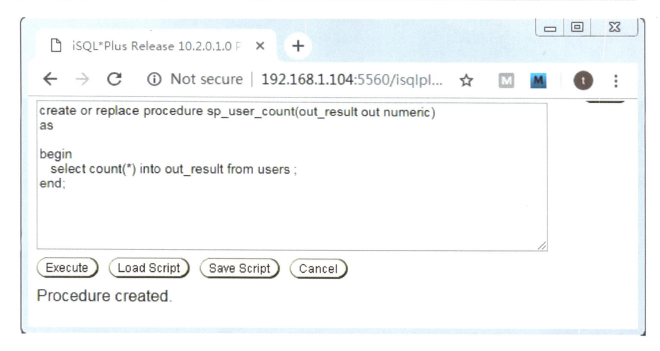

2. Calling a stored procedure : sp_user_count

```java
import java.sql.*;

public class TestAdd_Id {

    public static void main(String[] args) {

        DBUtil db = new DBUtil();
        Connection conn = db.openConnection();
        String sql = "call sp_user_count(?)";

        try {
            CallableStatement callStmt = conn.prepareCall(sql);
            callStmt.registerOutParameter(1, Types.INTEGER);
            callStmt.executeUpdate();

            int id = callStmt.getInt(1);
            System.out.println("users count : ' + id);

        } catch (SQLException e) {
            e.printStackTrace();
        }
    }
}
```

Result:

```
users count : 10
```

Thanks for learning

https://www.amazon.com/dp/B08HTXMXVY   https://www.amazon.com/dp/B086SPBJ87

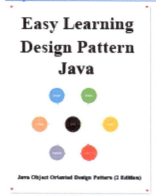

https://www.amazon.com/dp/B08BWT6RCT

If you enjoyed this book and found some benefit in reading this, I'd like to hear from you and hope that you could take some time to post a review on Amazon. Your feedback and support will help us to greatly improve in future and make this book even better.

You can follow this link now.

http://www.amazon.com/review/create-review?&asin=1095228676

I wish you all the best in your future success!